Design: Art of Design
Recipe Photography: Peter Barry
Jacket and Illustration Artwork: Jane Winton, courtesy
of Bernard Thornton Artists, London
Editors: Jillian Stewart and Kate Cranshaw

CLB 3520
Published by Grange Books, an imprint of Grange Books
PLC, The Grange, Grange Yard, London, SE1 3AG
© 1994 CLB Publishing, Godalming, Surrey, England.
Printed and bound in Singapore
Published in 1994
ISBN 1-85627-444-6

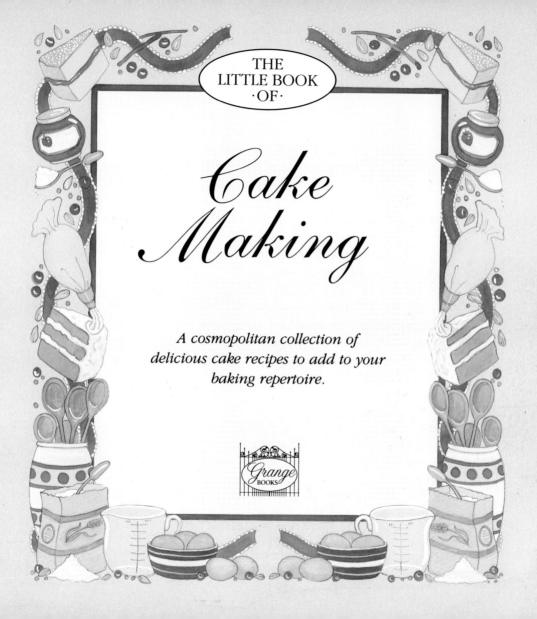

THE LITTLE BOOK ·OF·

Cake Making

A cosmopolitan collection of delicious cake recipes to add to your baking repertoire.

Grange BOOKS

Introduction

There is something of great social significance about cakes and cake making. Cakes are about occasions; they are to do with entertaining, enjoyment, indulgence. Cakes are about the good things in life. There are cakes for birthdays, for weddings, for christenings, and for anniversaries. There are cakes for Christmas and Easter and Halloween. There are cakes for the opening of plays, films and buildings, and for the launching of ships. And there are cakes simply to accompany coffee. A cake is always an indication of goodwill, of wanting to share, and of wanting to be sociable – and of course there is often an element of wanting to impress!

Cakes do not have to be ornate, although there is a great trend nowadays to decorate a cake into any one of a fantastic number of themes: fairytales, skating boots, cartoon characters for children's birthday parties, wedding cakes with tiny iced slippers representing the giving away of the bride. All these are fine, and particularly magnificent to look at, but often the energy and ingenuity spent on the decoration is greater than that devoted to the cake mixture. Such cakes can be too good to cut, and not good enough to eat!

The recipes here are about delicious ingredients and wholesome and mouthwatering tastes to be shared with friends and relations. Coffee breaks and tea-time are ideal times at

which to indulge in cake eating. These are both rather anachronistic in these modern times of calorie counting and weight watching, but life would be dull indeed if we did not give in to culinary temptations from time to time. It is surely far better to slice into a delicious homemade cake as a special treat than to resort, in a gnawing, hungry moment, to a clutch of chocolate bars. The secret is to plan your treats in advance, bake the chosen cake, and then to bring it out with a flourish to delight your family and friends at the time of need.

Cake making techniques and methods vary tremendously and, indeed, are also of social significance. A cake mixture can be rushed, literally in a minute or two, from food processor bowl into the oven. Modern pressures of work and family commitments, all to be squeezed into a day that is never long enough, are such that a cake is frequently thrown together in this way. The food processor's greatest use is probably for cake making. It is difficult, however, not to feel a certain nostalgia for those days when the only cake-making utensils were the wooden spoon and the stoneware mixing bowl. Of course, there are still plenty of people who make cakes in the traditional way. It is all a matter of personal preference, and how much time you have on your hands. It is nice, though, to think that a handmade cake has a little extra love and sympathy stirred into it.

Coconut Layer Cake

SERVES 6

The addition of coconut to this delicious cake helps to keep it moist.

PREPARATION: 20 mins
COOKING: 25 mins

225g/8oz butter
460g/1lb sugar
3 eggs, separated
340g/12oz flour
2 tsps baking powder
225ml/8 fl oz coconut milk
150g/5oz freshly grated coconut
Seedless raspberry jam

---

1. Cream together the butter and sugar in a mixing bowl until pale and fluffy. Beat in the egg yolks one by one, beating well after each addition.

2. Sift together the flour and the baking powder and fold into the butter mixture alternately with the coconut milk, stirring after each addition until the batter is smooth.

3. Stir in two thirds of the grated coconut. Whisk the egg whites until stiff then fold them gently into the cake batter.

4. Divide the batter between three greased sandwich tins and bake in an oven preheated to 180°C/350°F/Gas Mark 4, for about 25 minutes, or until springy to the touch. Turn out onto a wire rack to cool.

5. To assemble the cake, sandwich the layers together with the raspberry jam. Spread another layer of jam over the top of the cake and cover with the remaining coconut.

Almond Layer Gateau

MAKES ONE 20cm/8-INCH ROUND CAKE
Definitely not for the diet conscious, but delicious for those wishing to sin.

PREPARATION: 40 mins
COOKING: 35 mins

60g/2oz dried white breadcrumbs
120ml/4 fl oz milk
2 tbsps rum
90g/3oz unsalted butter or margarine
90g/3oz caster sugar
6 eggs, separated
90g/3oz roasted almonds, ground
570ml/1 pint double cream
2 tbsps icing sugar
60g/2oz roasted almonds, finely chopped
Whole blanched almonds, lightly toasted

---

1. Put the breadcrumbs into a large bowl and pour over the milk and half of the rum. Stand until the liquid has been completely absorbed.

2. Beat the butter in a large bowl until soft. Gradually add the sugar, mixing until light and fluffy. Beat in the egg yolks, one at a time mixing well. Fold in the breadcrumbs.

3. Whisk the egg whites until stiff, but not dry. Fold into the mixture with the ground almonds.

Step 2 Beat the egg yolks, one at a time, into the butter and sugar mixture, mixing well to prevent curdling.

4. Divide the cake mixture equally between 3 × 20cm/8-inch round cake tins; all greased, floured and lined. Bake in an oven preheated to 180°C/350°F/Gas Mark 4, for 30-35 minutes, until well risen and golden. Cool briefly before turning onto a wire rack.

5. Whip the cream until stiff, then beat in the icing sugar and remaining rum. Reserve one third of the cream and fold the finely chopped almonds into the rest.

6. Sandwich the cake layers together with the almond cream, then spread the plain cream onto the top, reserving some for piping. Decorate with the toasted whole almonds.

Guinness Cake

Guinness adds a lovely flavour to this rich fruit cake.

PREPARATION: 25 mins
COOKING: 2 hrs

225g/8oz butter or margarine
225g/8oz brown sugar
340ml/12 fl oz Guinness
225g/8oz raisins
225g/8oz currants
225g/8oz sultanas
120g/4oz chopped mixed peel
570g/1¼lbs plain flour
1 tsp allspice
1 tsp nutmeg
½ tsp bicarbonate of soda
3 eggs, beaten

---

1. Place the butter, sugar and the Guinness in a saucepan and bring slowly to the boil, stirring constantly until the sugar and butter have melted.

2. Mix in the dried fruit and peel and bring the mixture back to the boil, then simmer for 5 minutes. Remove from the heat and cool thoroughly.

3. Sift the flour, spices and bicarbonate of soda into a large mixing bowl. Stir in the cooled fruit mixture and add the beaten eggs.

4. Turn into a greased and lined deep 23cm/9-inch cake tin and bake in the centre of an oven preheated to 160°C/325°F/Gas Mark 3, for 2 hours or until a skewer inserted in the centre comes out clean. When done, cool in the tin before removing to a cake rack.

Saffron Babas

MAKES 2 CAKES

This is a traditional Polish Easter cake. Cooks spoke in whispers when these cakes were cooling since loud noise was believed to damage the delicate texture!

PREPARATION: 2 hrs
COOKING: 40-50 mins

275g/10oz plain flour
420ml/¾ pint lukewarm milk
90g/3oz fresh yeast
175g/6oz sugar
4 eggs plus 4 yolks
Grated rind of 1 lemon
3 tbsps brandy
Pinch powdered saffron
900g/2lbs plain flour
Pinch salt
175g/6oz melted butter, slightly cooled
120g/4oz raisins
2 tbsps chopped mixed peel

1. First prepare a 'sponge' with the 300g/10oz flour. Blend the milk and yeast together and pour into a well in the centre of the flour. Mix with a wooden spoon and cover.

2. Leave in a warm place for about 1 hour, until it doubles in bulk and the top becomes bubbly and spongy.

3. Combine the sugar together with the eggs and egg yolks, lemon rind, brandy and saffron. Mix with the flour mixture and add the

Step 4 Leave the dough to rise a second time in the cake tins until completely filled.

remaining flour and salt. Knead by hand for about 30 minutes in the bowl or on a very well-floured surface.

4. Place the dough back in the bowl and add the butter, raisins and peel. Knead until it is smooth and elastic and does not stick. Divide in 2 equal portions. Butter two 25cm/10-inch round cake tins very thickly and place in the dough, patting it out evenly. Cover each with lightly-oiled clingfilm and put in a warm place to rise until the tins are filled.

5. Bake in an oven preheated to 200°C/400°F/ Gas Mark 6 for about 40-50 minutes, or until a skewer inserted into the centre of each comes out clean. Leave to cool in the tins for about 10-14 minutes and then remove to a cooling rack. Sprinkle with sugar or drizzle with icing.

Poppy Seed Cake

SERVES 6-8

This is the Christmas version of an ever popular Polish cake.

PREPARATION: 1 hr
COOKING: 45-50 mins

Dough
90g/3oz butter or margarine
90g/3oz sugar
1 egg
45-60ml/3-4 tbsps lukewarm milk
1½ tbsps dried yeast
340g/12oz plain flour

Filling
200ml/7 fl oz milk
120g/4oz poppy seeds
45g/1½oz butter or margarine
75ml/5 tbsps honey
2 tbsps ground walnuts
45g/1½oz raisins
1 tbsp finely chopped glacé peel
1 egg
60g/2oz sugar
3 tbsps brandy

1. To prepare the dough, cream the butter with the sugar until light and fluffy and gradually add the egg, beating in well. Add a pinch of salt. Dissolve the yeast in the milk and add to the other ingredients. Sift in the flour and mix to a dough. Knead well until smooth and elastic.

2. To test if the dough has been sufficiently kneaded, press lightly – if it springs back fairly quickly, it is ready to leave to rise.

3. Place the dough in a lightly greased bowl, cover with a damp cloth and leave in a warm place for about 1 hour, or until doubled in bulk.

4. For the filling, boil the milk then add the poppy seeds. Cook over low heat for about 30 minutes, stirring frequently. Drain the seeds well and blend to a paste in a liquidiser.

5. Melt the butter and add the honey, walnuts, raisins and peel. Add the seed paste and cook for about 15 minutes, stirring frequently over moderate heat.

6. Beat the egg with the sugar until light and fluffy and add to the seed mixture. Cook over gentle heat, stirring constantly to thicken. Add the brandy and set aside.

7. When the dough has doubled in bulk, knock it back and knead for a further 2-5 minutes. Roll out thinly on a floured surface, shaping it into a rectangle. Spread the filling evenly over it and roll up tightly as for a Swiss roll, pressing the ends together to seal. Place on a lightly buttered baking sheet curving into a horse shoe. Bake in an oven preheated to 190°C/375°F/Gas Mark 5, for 45-50 minutes, or until golden brown. Serve plain or with icing.

Irish Coffee Cake

SERVES 8

This is a delicious cake flavoured with Irish whiskey and covered with whipped cream.

PREPARATION: 30 mins
COOKING: 35-40 mins

120g/4oz butter or margarine
120g/4oz caster sugar
2 eggs
120g/4oz plain flour
1 tsp baking powder
2 tsps instant coffee dissolved in 2 tbsps hot
    water

Syrup
120g/4oz sugar
175ml/6 fl oz strong coffee
3 tbsps Irish whiskey

Topping
140ml/¼ pint whipping cream
1 heaped tbsp icing sugar
1 tbsp Irish whiskey
Whole hazelnuts

---

1. In a bowl, cream together the butter and sugar until light and fluffy, then add the eggs one at a time beating in well.

2. Sift the flour and baking powder together and fold two-thirds of it into the creamed mixture using a metal spoon. Add the dissolved coffee and mix in well. Fold in the remainder of the flour.

3. Place in a greased and floured 20cm/8-inch ring tin and bake in an oven preheated to 180°C/350°F/Gas Mark 4, for 35-40 minutes, or until a skewer comes out clean when inserted in the middle. Turn out onto a wire rack to cool.

4. To make the syrup, heat the sugar in the coffee until dissolved then boil rapidly for 1 minute. Remove from the heat and beat in the whiskey.

5. Return the cooled cake to the well-washed tin and pour the syrup over it. Leave it to soak for several hours.

6. Beat the cream with the icing sugar and whiskey. Turn the cake out onto a serving plate and decorate with the cream and whole hazelnuts. Chill before serving.

Syrup Cake

SERVES 8

Rather like gingerbread this cake can be served with coffee, or warm with cream as a pudding.

PREPARATION: 20 mins
COOKING: 45 mins

225g/8oz white vegetable fat
225ml/8 fl oz treacle
3 eggs, beaten
340g/12oz plain flour
Pinch salt
1 tbsp baking powder
1 tsp cinnamon
¼ tsp ground nutmeg
Pinch ground cloves
30g/4 tbsps chopped nuts
45g/4 tbsps raisins

---

1. Cream the fat until light and fluffy. Add the

Step 1 Cream the fat until light and fluffy. Beat in the treacle with an electric mixer.

Step 2 Sift in the dry ingredients and combine by hand.

treacle and beat with an electric mixer. Add the eggs one at a time, beating well in between each addition.

2. Sift the flour together with a pinch of salt, the baking powder and spices. Fold into the treacle mixture.

3. Stir in the nuts and raisins and pour the mixture into a lightly greased 13.5 × 32.5cm/ 9 × 13 inch baking tin.

4. Bake in an oven preheated to 190°C/375°F/ Gas Mark 5 for about 45 minutes, or until a skewer inserted into the centre of the cake comes out clean. Allow to cool and cut into squares to serve.

Victoria Sandwich Cake

SERVES 6-8

This is the classic cake to serve for afternoon tea.

PREPARATION: 20 mins
COOKING: 25 mins

120g/4oz butter or margarine
120g/4oz caster sugar
2 large eggs
Few drops vanilla essence
120g/4oz self-raising flour, sifted

To finish
Jam, whipped cream and sifted icing sugar

---

1. In a medium-sized mixing bowl, cream together the butter and sugar until light and fluffy. Beat in the eggs one at a time and the vanilla essence.

2. With a metal spoon, gently fold in the sifted flour. When it is all incorporated, divide the mixture equally between two greased and lined 18cm/7-inch sandwich tins, levelling off the surface.

3. Bake in the centre of an oven preheated to 180°C/350°F/Gas Mark 4, for about 25 minutes. Test by pressing your finger gently onto the sponge, it should feel springy and leave no impression when the cake is done.

4. Leave to cool for a minute in the tins, then turn out onto wire cooling racks and carefully peel off the greaseproof paper.

5. When cold, sandwich together with jam and whipped cream and dust the top with sifted icing sugar.

Christmas Cake

MAKES ONE 23cm/9-INCH SQUARE CAKE

Although this fruit cake is made without eggs and sugar, it is still rich and moist.

PREPARATION: 40 mins
COOKING: 3¼-3½ hrs

120ml/4 fl oz clear honey
175ml/6 fl oz safflower or sunflower oil
90g/3oz soya flour
280ml/½ pint water
1 tbsp rum or 1 tsp rum essence
Grated rind and juice of 1 orange
Grated rind and juice of 1 lemon
60g/2oz flaked almonds
90g/3oz dried figs, chopped
90g/3oz dried dates, chopped
60g/2oz dried apricots, chopped
225g/8oz wholewheat self-raising flour
Pinch salt
2 tsps mixed spice
225g/8oz currants
225g/8oz sultanas
225g/8oz raisins

---

1. Cream the honey and the oil together.

2. Mix the soya flour with the water and gradually add to the oil and honey mixture, beating well.

3. Beat in the rum and the grated rind and juice of the orange and lemon. Add the almonds, figs, dates and apricots.

4. Mix the wholewheat flour with the salt and spice and mix together the currants, sultanas and raisins.

5. Stir half the flour and half the currant mixture into the soya cream, then stir in the remainder. Spoon into a greased and lined deep 23cm/9-inch square cake tin.

6. Cover with two or three layers of brown paper and bake in an oven preheated to 170°C/325°F/Gas Mark 3, for 3¼-3½ hours, or until a skewer inserted into the centre comes out clean.

7. Cool for 10 minutes in the tin, then turn out onto a wire rack to cool completely. Store for 3-4 weeks in an airtight tin wrapped in greaseproof paper, before cutting.

Kugelhopf

SERVES 8

This Continental yeasted cake is ideal for serving at teatime.

PREPARATION: 40 mins, plus 2 hrs proving
COOKING: 45 mins

520g/1lb 2oz plain flour
225ml/8 fl oz warm milk
4 tsps yeast
2 tbsps plum liqueur
90g/3oz raisins
¼ tsp salt
2 eggs
120g/4oz sugar
175g/6oz butter, softened
5 tbsps slivered almonds

1. Mix together 75g/2½oz of the flour with half the warm milk and all the yeast and leave for 1

Step 2 Knead the dough in the bowl using your hands, for at least 5 minutes.

Step 4 When the dough has tripled in volume mix in the raisins and almonds.

hour in a warm place. Pour the liqueur over the raisins and leave to soak.

2. Mix the salt, eggs, sugar and remaining milk into the remaining flour. Knead the dough for at least 5 minutes in the bowl with your hands.

3. Knead in the softened butter and the yeast mixture until well mixed, then set the dough aside in a warm place for 1 hour, or until tripled in volume.

4. When the dough has tripled in size, mix in the raisins and almonds. Place in a greased kugelhopf, or brioche mould and bake in an oven preheated to 180°C/350°F/Gas Mark 4, for 45 minutes. Allow to rest in the tin for 15 minutes before turning out.

Sour Cream Cake

SERVES 8-10

An extremely moreish cake from across the Atlantic. More or less cinnamon can be added as preferred.

PREPARATION: 20 mins
COOKING: 40 mins

120g/4oz butter
200g/7oz sugar
2 eggs
150ml/5 fl oz carton soured cream
1 tsp bicarbonate of soda
175g/6oz plain flour
1½ tsps baking powder
1 tsp vanilla essence

Topping
60g/2oz demerara sugar
2 tbsps chopped mixed nuts
2 tsps cinnamon

---

1. In a large bowl, cream together the butter and sugar until light and fluffy.

2. Beat in the eggs and soured cream mixed with the bicarbonate of soda. Blend well.

3. Sieve together the flour and baking powder and fold in gently using a metal spoon. Add the vanilla.

4. Mix all the topping ingredients together. Pour half the cake mixture into a greased 23cm/9-inch ring tin and sprinkle with half the topping.

5. Pour in the remaining mixture and sprinkle with the rest of the topping.

6. Bake in an oven preheated to 180°C/350°F/ Gas Mark 4, for 40 minutes or until risen and springy to the touch.

Carrot Cake with Apricot Filling

SERVES 6-8

This tasty cake will freeze well for up to 2 months.

PREPARATION: 20 mins
COOKING: 45-50 mins

120g/4oz dried apricots
175g/6oz butter or margarine
175g/6oz brown sugar
2 eggs, separated
200g/7oz plain flour
1 tsp baking powder
225g/8oz carrots (150g/5oz weight when
    peeled and finely grated)
60g/2oz sultanas
90g/3oz walnuts, finely chopped
2 tsps grated lemon rind
½ tsp ground cinnamon

---

1. Soak the apricots in water overnight, drain and purée until smooth.

2. Beat the butter and sugar together until pale and creamy.

3. Whisk the egg yolks and beat into the butter and sugar.

4. Sieve the flour and baking powder and fold into the mixture.

5. Fold in the rest of the ingredients except the egg whites.

6. Whisk the egg whites until they form soft peaks, and fold into the mixture.

7. Place the mixture in a greased 18cm/7-inch round spring-form cake tin. Bake in an oven preheated to 180°C/350°F/Gas Mark 4, for 45-50 minutes.

8. Cool in the tin for 10 minutes and then turn out onto a wire rack.

9. When completely cooled, slice in half and sandwich together with the apricot purée.

Praline Sponge Cake

SERVES 4

This extravagant dessert cake is well worth its slightly time-consuming assembly and will earn you many compliments. Praline can be bought from specialist cake shops.

PREPARATION: 1 hr 30 mins
COOKING: 25 mins

4 eggs
175g/6oz sugar
175g/6oz plain flour, sifted
30g/1oz butter, melted

Praline cream filling
1 tbsp powdered gelatine
75g/5½ tbsps sugar
3 egg yolks
4 tsps flour
460ml/16 fl oz milk
75g/5½ tbsps praline
175ml/6 fl oz double cream
2 tbsps crushed praline
Whipped cream and crushed praline, to decorate

Step 1 Beat the eggs and sugar over a pan of simmering water.

minutes, or until springy to the touch. Turn out onto a wire rack and allow to cool, then slice into four layers.

3. To make the filling, dissolve the gelatine in a little hot water. Mix the sugar, egg yolks and flour together. Bring the milk to the boil with the praline, stirring to dissolve, then pour over the egg yolk mixture, and mix together well. Return to the pan and stir over a low heat until thickened. Stir in the gelatine, then allow to cool for 15 minutes, stirring occasionally.

4. Whip the cream until stiff, then fold it gently but thoroughly into the filling, together with the crushed praline.

5. Layer up the sponge and filling, using a palette knife to spread the last quarter of filling over the top and sides of the cake. Chill for 2 hours before serving, then decorate with whipped cream and crushed praline.

1. In a bowl, beat the eggs and sugar over a pan of simmering water until pale and thick. Remove the bowl and continue to beat until cooled and the mixture forms ribbons when dropped from a whisk.

2. Gently fold in the flour and the melted butter, then three quarters-fill a greased and floured deep cake tin. Bake in an oven preheated to 160°C/325°F/Gas Mark 3, for 25

Redcurrant Griestorte

SERVES 6

This light, delicious cake would taste equally good if filled with other fruit such as raspberries or blueberries.

PREPARATION: 20 mins
COOKING: 30 mins

Small amount of caster sugar and flour
3 large eggs, separated
150g/5oz caster sugar
Grated rind and juice of 1 lemon
1 tbsp ground almonds
60g/2oz fine semolina
140ml/¼ pint double cream
1 tbsp milk
120g/4oz redcurrants
Icing sugar

---

1. Line a 20 × 30cm/8 × 12 inch Swiss roll tin with non-stick paper, making a collar that stands up above the rim. Butter the paper and sprinkle with a little caster sugar and a dusting of flour.

2. In a bowl, whisk the egg yolks with the sugar until pale, thick and creamy. Whisk in the lemon juice. Combine ground almonds, semolina and lemon rind and carefully stir into the mixture.

3. Whisk the egg whites until stiff, then fold egg yolk mixture gently through the egg whites. Turn into the prepared tin. Bake in an oven preheated to 180°C/350°F/Gas Mark 4, for about 30 minutes until risen, pale golden brown and springy to the touch.

4. Turn out carefully onto a sheet of non-stick paper dusted with caster sugar. Trim the edges if necessary, then roll up loosely with some non-stick paper inside, and leave to cool on a wire rack.

5. Whisk together the cream and milk until fairly stiff. Unroll the cake, spread with the cream and sprinkle with the redcurrants, reserving some for decoration. Roll up, dust with icing sugar and decorate with the reserved fruit.

Pineapple Upside-Down Cake

SERVES 6

This old favourite makes an ideal pudding on a cold winter's day.

PREPARATION: 30 mins
COOKING: 45 mins

2 large eggs
120g/4oz butter or margarine
120g/4oz caster sugar
90g/3oz self-raising flour
30g/1oz ground almonds
2 tbsps milk
½ tsp vanilla essence
Few drops almond essence

Topping
Small can pineapple rings, drained and halved
30g/1oz butter
30g/1oz demerara sugar
30-60g/1-2oz glacé cherries, halved

1. Cream the butter and sugar until light and fluffy. Beat the eggs lightly and gradually add to the creamed mixture together with the essences.

2. Sieve the flour, stir in ground almonds and fold into the mixture using a metal tablespoon. Add the milk to make a soft batter consistency.

3. Melt the butter for the topping in a 20cm/8-inch square cake tin or an 18cm/7-inch round tin and use to grease the sides.

4. Sprinkle the demerara sugar over the melted butter. Arrange the pineapple halves on the sugared base and decorate with the cherries.

5. Carefully spread the cake mixture on top of the fruit. Bake in an oven preheated to 190°C/375°F/Gas Mark 5, for 45 minutes. Remove from the oven, loosen the sides with a knife and turn out onto a warmed dish.

6. Serve either with custard or cream, or make a sauce made from the pineapple juice – thicken with 2 tsps of cornflour and boil for 2-3 minutes; sweeten to taste.

Pound Cake

SERVES 8

This is a plain cake that complements fruit salads to perfection, and is also a welcome addition to the afternoon tea table.

PREPARATION: 20 mins
COOKING: 45 mins

340g/12oz softened unsalted butter
340g/12oz caster sugar
5 eggs
½ tsp vanilla essence, or 2 tsps orange
  flower water
2 tsps baking powder
340g/12oz flour

Step 3 Spoon the batter into a non-stick loaf tin.

1. In a large mixing bowl cream together the butter and sugar until light and fluffy.

Step 3 Fold in the sieved flour and baking powder.

2. Beat in the eggs one at a time, together with the vanilla or orange flower water. Beat well between each addition to ensure that the egg is fully incorporated before adding more; this will prevent the mixture from curdling.

3. Sift the baking powder with the flour then fold into the mixture to obtain a thick batter. Spoon the cake batter into either a non-stick or a greased and lined loaf tin.

4. Bake in an oven preheated to 180°C/350°F/ Gas Mark 4, for about 45 minutes, or until a skewer inserted in the centre of the cake comes out clean. Turn out onto a wire rack to cool.

Apple Cake

SERVES 8

Serve this delicious cake warm with apple purée and cream or custard.

PREPARATION: 20 mins
COOKING: 45 mins

---

1 tsp cinnamon
175g/6oz self-raising flour
175g/6oz butter or margarine
175g/6oz caster sugar
3 eggs
2 tbsps milk
2-3 eating apples, peeled, cored and thinly
   sliced

---

1. Add the cinnamon to the flour and sift into a bowl. Cream butter and sugar until pale and fluffy.

2. Beat in the eggs one at a time, adding 1 tbsp of the flour after each. Fold in two-thirds of the remaining flour, then stir in the milk, before folding in the last of the flour.

3. Grease a 28 × 22cm/11 × 8½ inch baking dish. Spread half the batter in the bottom, distribute the apple slices over it and cover with the rest of the batter.

4. Bake in an oven preheated to 180°C/350°F/Gas Mark 4, for 15 minutes then reduce heat to 160°C/325°F/Gas Mark 3, and continue baking for 30 minutes until golden brown and firm to the touch.

Lemon Cake

SERVES 6-8

This cake would work equally well if orange was substituted for the lemon.

PREPARATION: 15 mins
COOKING: 45 mins

120g/4oz butter
225g/8oz sugar
1 lemon
2 eggs, separated
225g/8oz flour
1½ tsps baking powder
120ml/4 fl oz milk

---

1. Cream together the butter and sugar until pale and fluffy. Grate the rind of the lemon and beat in along with 2 tsps of the juice. Beat in the egg yolks one at a time.

2. Sift together the flour and the baking powder and add to the butter mixture in batches alternately with the milk. Beat well after each addition to obtain a smooth batter.

3. Whisk the egg whites until stiff and fold them gently into the cake batter.

4. Turn the batter into a greased cake tin, and bake in an oven preheated to 180°C/350°F/Gas Mark 4, for 45 minutes, or until springy to the touch. Turn out onto a cake rack and leave to cool.

5. The cake can be split, and sandwiched together with lemon curd and dusted with icing sugar on the top.

Index